Moments
and
Fantasies

Moments and Fantasies

Ole Eddie Kane The Next Generation

authorHOUSE®

AuthorHouse™
1663 Liberty Drive
Bloomington, IN 47403
www.authorhouse.com
Phone: 1-800-839-8640

First published by AuthorHouse   02/24/2012

ISBN: 978-1-4685-5668-1 (sc)
ISBN: 978-1-4685-5669-8 (hc)
ISBN: 978-1-4685-5670-4 (ebk)

Library of Congress Control Number: 2012903375

Printed in the United States of America

INTRODUCTION

What do you want to know about me?! If I told you that I was raised by two very strong black women an influenced by many people!! Would that give you an opinion or judgment of who I am as a black hueMAN?! Let me help you out, Ole Eddie Kane The Next Generation ain't Sugar Honey Iced Tea! This way you can't say I didn't warn you up front! As you read, use your imagination to understand the natural flow of my mood! Ladies it ain't your booty any more, it's that overall beauty that each of you possess that I see and look for. That thing that makes you more than just Sexy but DESIRABLE! Let me show you, so that you know no matter what, you are DESIRED! Can I be that FRIEND you need to fulfill a want?! And the want that needs fulfilling by a FRIEND! No more, no less! Just think, I wrote this on my cell phone on Feb. 2nd. 2012 at 11:43am! What were you doing?!

ACKNOWLEDGEMENTS

To my Friend who suggested to me that I write out my thoughts in the year 2009 that led me to this, I thank you very much! Now do you believe me?! My Brother that believed in me enough to invest in my dream, thank you very much also! To my co-worker who took the time to help me in the beginning stages, thank you and I got you! To those who had no Faith in me, I'm not mad at all! Disappointed yes, but I thank you any way because it was your lack of Faith that focused my determination to get this done. An to the ladies, thank you for just being you! As you read I hope you can find your self in my words, because this is for you!! Ole Eddie Kane, The Next Generation

A FIRST DATE

If there's a spark, shouldn't we be able to touch? An innocent gesture? What about chemistry? If we have that couldn't that gesture be a little more flirtatious? Now what if there's fire that leads to a passionate kiss! We have all that in one place between you and I. Can we kiss touch and caress each other until my pants are stained to the right?! And you look like you've peed on yourself. Now that's what I call a first date. We get into our own showers only to masturbate thinking of one another. As we begin to moisturize our bodies, flashes of what we shared flow through our minds, descriptions of our naked oiled bodies through Bluetooth stimulate the senses even more. Now I've arrived . . . . literally! Did you? If you feel my flow then you know I'm thinking about chu! Not you, chu! Who is reading this? Remember me, you saw me at?!

STOP LIGHT

Damn, you were sexy standing there! What you had on turned me on more than anything else. Everything fit and looked so good on you. I know anybody else could've had that same thing on too! But at this very MOMENT, you are the finest motherfucker I've seen in ages. Looking at you, the desire to bathe you in my flow was all I thought about. A flow of passion where I project what I felt about you in that MOMENT, to caress your clothed body, stroke your face, hair and dive into your eyes. Then the light changed and you were occupied with your cell phone. Our eyes never met, but thank you for that "MOMENT."

THEM LIPS

Your lips were the first thing I saw—yes that was all it took to catch my eye. You might not have noticed my stare but my MOMENT started there. Kissing your lips with a deep seeded passion and a desire that could only be satisfied by the connection of our lips, tongues and tongue rings. Arms embraced, bodies touching, fingers playing on skin and hair, breathing slowed to one breathe and seconds seem like hours. The thirst that you provided and quenched with one kiss is over. We wipe the corners of our mouths, no need to talk, your lips provided that MOMENT.

THE BEGINNING

The first time I did it was on a dare. She thought I wouldn't go through with it. I won't lie, I had no clue as to what to do but for some reason it was very clear. Maybe she knew what she was doing, but I didn't, unafraid to take the dare, it began from that point many years ago. Blame her or thank her, but it was her that sparked the passion. I licked her pussy unsure of what I was doing. Then I hit something with my tongue that got a strange reaction from her. Her body jerked like someone hit her in the throat, then after she regained her breathe she moaned like something rippled through her body. I felt like I had discovered something powerful! Something that drove me to attack that specific spot. I ran my tongue over that button (clit) so many ways causing her to breathe rapidly. The more I licked, sucked, flicked, kissed, teased and just for the lack of a better word, PULVERIZED her clit. We started in the middle of the living room and she ended up with her back on the stairs. She lay there unable or unwilling to move, she was spent. When she was able to move, she put her panties back on, pulled her skirt down and left. I have not seen her since. Thanks for the beginning of the Bearded Clan Clit Lickers MOMENT.

ONE HELL OF A NIGHT

That night was already passionate, but the MOMENT hit when she kneeled facing the window on that black leather couch. Candles lit the room as the moon lit the sky. Her hair fell down to the center of her back, ass upward begging for a lick. I pulled her hair to one side and I ran my tongue from her kitchen all the way to the crack of her ass . . . slowly. Her pussy was dripping, yearning for the touch of my tongue and what do you think she got? Hmmmmm?! If you thought tongue, then you'd be correct. Oh yes, down right nasty, her salad was tossed just to make her pussy cum. I laid on my back; she sat down and the TONGUE FU began. My ability to suck her clit and lick her pussy walls at the same time. I held her clit in my mouth and licked around that sweet juicy hole. Sometimes putting the tip in and out of her. What she felt was only expressed by her screaming, cussing, moaning, groaning, crying and the pressing need to get my tongue deeper inside of her. My hands massaged her large succulent breasts, squeezing the nipples towards her drooling mouth and tongue. She was grinding, jerking and twitching her pussy over my chin, lips, tongue, nose, and forehead and then she stopped. I didn't, but she did. My arms were tested, locked around her legs, but tested. If I could've been a fly on the wall, her head flew back and her body followed half way. She then rocked forward all the way at that time, I was flat tongued and licked her pussy up to her clit. She rose up forcefully trying to escape her forthcoming nut (climax, if you prefer). My arms gave very little. There was an escape try with one last effort, only to come down forcing my tongue deeper into her sweet tunnel. Within a split second, she shot forward like something hot touched her. Hands gripping the couch, cheeks pressed against the window, hips popping, knees buckling and pussy mmmmmm . . . !!! It had a heart beat y'all. Her eyes are shut tight and her mouth was opening and closing an who knows what between breaths. Are you in her MOMENT! Me too. From where I stood, my MOMENT continued the way she was positioned.

ONE HELL OF A NIGHT PART 2

The atmosphere at that very MOMENT was nothing outside that room mattered. My tongue twitched when my eyes focused on her asshole with her finger in it. Yeah, who wouldn't notice that! I had lubrication close by and she wanted to try something new. No words were needed or uttered. The head was ready for slow, gentle penetration into her ass. The tip pushed slowly through. She tried to relax; her body tensed but was adjusting. The new sensations she felt, the more her ass relaxed, the deeper she pushed back onto me. She reached her fill, relaxing and gently squeezing her muscles around me. One hand on my chest and the other squeezing her breast like a vice grip. Her face was distorted by pains of pleasures and pleasures of pain. Damn, don't describe shit do it? It was tighter than freshly douched pussy, mmm. That one tensed my body thinking about that MOMENT!! Oh yeah, this is my views and fantasies!!! I ease in and out slowly for both our pleasures. My hands on her hips controlled her motions somewhat and the moans did the rest. I couldn't count them because I had something to do. Ooh, it felt so good, but unless I meet a WOMAN that can take a dick in her ass like her I'll stay in the pussy, THANK YOU. Now for some reason, it started to thunder and lightning through the night sky. Ever so often when I went to slam forward and pull her back, thunder would shake the room. She cried out in pleasure, pussy juices running down both legs. I could feel the surge building in me and I slowed my violent pace. That made the surge greater feeling my movement she knew what was coming (me). She thrust back hard and knowing her, I caught some of her force. But the way her ass moved when she hit my shaved pubic area, it stimulated every muscle at once. (Sorry had to touch myself briefly). She thrust back once more and every pore, nose, ears, and mouth opened at once. When I released my hand, I had a grip on her hair and one gripping her breast; she bucked violently when she felt those hot spurts shoot inside her. Just as I had, she did too. The way I held her, all she could do was feel my flow mix with her own. Her muscles locked down holding my still hard dick in place as it jerked and twitched as her juices flowed to the couch. Time didn't exist holding her body, in the night air. That changed when the rain cooled air brushed past our sweat and fluid covered bodies. My hard dick flicked the bottom of her pussy coming out causing her to buck. With grace and poise, she turned, took my dick in her hand, gently sliding me into her mouth totally. My knees buckled and with no mercy, she attacked. My dick was shown the same mercy she had endured. Sucking with force, unrelenting to my pleads of mercy, she didn't stop. (Some may say, you acting like a bitch, Man up. Fuck Y'all) Like some men after a nut like that, a deep coma like sleep would be next. That would've been good, but she had very different plans. Assault charges being pressed crossed my mind, as she used her hands, teeth, tongue, saliva, and throat with precision and accuracy until her goal was achieved.

THAT TIME OF THE MONTH

Baby, I don't give a fuck if you're bleeding, your clit is the only thing I need. I'm no old raisin. Right for the money, your clit, baby girl, is what I'm here for honey. Now some men don't go there that time of the month, when the pussy's shut down and they can't get none. Selfish thinking if you ask me. She can bust a nut without using, the dick. Didn't you know or did you disregard the memo. Now after an argument about some dumb shit, push her down, lick her clit, and after she bust a nut, say, "Shut up Bitch."

WHEN TONGUES ATTACK

I walked into her bedroom, fresh from the shower, body still damp from the baby oil, looked down at her half asleep face and asked her how many she wanted? A look of curiosity and confusion as her head rose from the pillow. I repeated it again, "How many do you want?" She still had the same look on her face. With a look of "Oh, you forgot," I smoothly said, "Oh, you thought I was playing before I got in the shower about how many nuts you want to bust when I eat the pussy?" Her expression was like you bullshitting stupid ass, but I was not playing. A Moment When Tongues Attack. Are you ready for this?

Come on now, stop playing. I got shit to do! Take a shower after I am done, let's go is what I said, cause she still had that look on her face. She took her panties off as I nakedly walked to the other side of the bed. My mind was only locked to one thing . . . how many? So how many, one or two I asked. She replied one good one! With that the Tongue Attack began.

I slid under the sheet and comforter spreading her legs gently. Already lying on the pillows she readjusted for maximum comfort. The tip of my tongue touched the outer walls of her pussy. A very slight moan and twitch like a static shock through her body as I ran my tongue around her lips. Heavy breathing and deep sexy moans of pleasure muffled by the sheets and comforter urged me to lick more.

She was wet but that was just the beginning. Sometimes I wonder about this thing I have with oral facilitation of female pleasure. In layman's terms, I like eating pussy! What's there to wonder you ask? Well eating pussy gets me excited mentally, knowing that she busts as many nuts as she can just with my tongue, mmm. That's my thrill. Don't get it fucked up, the in and out (stroke) is great. But my focus is giving that woman as many screaming, cussing, fussing nuts as she can stand. My hands and arms were locked in place so she couldn't escape form that ONE she wanted. The hoop on my tongue ring was crossing her button, and then the tip of my tongue was driving all her senses crazy. Tongue Fu, when a man knows how to stimulate the button unjustly to bring an orgasm that makes her body arch to escape the inevitable. Though arched up, the button could not escape. Her body tensed up, breathing stopped at the point, she was in her MOMENT.

Do you remember yours?!

A LITTLE INSIGHT

No woman has ever compared to another. They've all had their own intriguing little way about them, individuals oh so very sexy in their own way. That's what attracts my flow, the flow of beautiful moments captured and shared for others to relate, reminisce and feel as someone else does. The natural flow of my mood is you feeling me or what? See as I see!

These Moments I share with you have some truth to them, but not all, they are a connection of Moments and Fantasies. Imagine what you read. Fill in some spots with your own imagination. Let your mind feel what I felt with each Moment.

OLD SCHOOL NECKING

We were in her apartment; the candle light was very seductive. I could not tell you if we were sipping wine or not because the music was intoxicating. The greatest hits from the Maestro himself, Barry White was playing. We about to go there, yes we is. Sex would have spoiled the night. Yes, it would. Shut up and keep reading. Not every Moment requires sex. This was foreplay at its best. Bodies were touched, caressed, and rubbed. The only that was penetrated was her mouth and ears, all by my tongue. Her pants were unbuttoned but not removed. The touch of another person can be very seductive, staring into each other's eyes, finding that spot, mmm! You like that huh? Yeah, me too.

My tongue traced her ear, lightly, slowly, listening for the reactions from blowing in her ear. She moaned softly. I blew again and then I said, "like that?" She slowly pulled away only to have my tongue lick across her inner ear causing her to twitch and moan. "Don't run," I said with a sexy smirk. I knew she was wet just by her look. We don't have to take our clothes completely off.

I love foreplay, getting to use my fingers, lips, and tongue. Touching her from the top of her head to her pant covered ass. Barry crooned, as the music itself carried us to a place of exploration of pleasures above the waist. Think about it, 'Old School Necking.' The CD stopped, the candles were half melted and the incense smell was faint. We were deeply embraced, lost in each other's connected skin. Her nipples were so erect and so were mine too for that matter. Her panties were soaked, as were her pants and the rug. My dick was so hard that the bitch hurt. We stood up, she zipped up her pants and I put my shirt on and adjusted my dick. We hugged deeply and she thanked me for taking her back to a time where sex wasn't the goal but foreplay was. A back in the day MOMENT.

SOMETHING YOU SHOULD KNOW

Ladies . . . , it's not that I'm not interested in having sex. It's just that I believe there's more to it. I want you to not only be satisfied sexually but mentally as well. A mental orgasm! Think of me as you read as I of you. How the contours of your body would feel with my fingers and hands. The clothes that you wore, how the fabric felt. Your lips, how they felt and tasted. Your neck, how it smelled, felt and tasted. Your hair, its texture, style, and smell. Your ears, to whisper how sexy you are and other nasty things to you. To do what you like to make you hot. Now if you didn't take a deep breathe a few times reading this then wait till you read some more. If you did then you have had a few mental orgasms. Good for you. Now just imagine what the possibilities that could be if I was really there with you lady?!

KEEP THIS IN MIND

After I lick the kitty it's on over to fill the hole. Now a seven pound baby dropped out of there. And let's just be clear my thing doesn't weigh seven pounds or even one. I'm not here to fill the hole; I'm HERE TO BREAK THE DAM!!!!

MS. ENTERTAINMENT

I've seen you many times in porn movies; the things that you did some would consider unpleasant, but who are they to judge? In my eyes you're still a very sexy lady. Seeing you in those movies always gets me to wondering have you ever felt a passion unlike nothing that you've ever had before. Imagine after a scene with you and some dudes, you wash up and still feel like there is something missing. That need that wasn't fulfilled and that want that you need fulfilled. Yes, the focus of you, your pleasure alone. That moment when your body melts with touches of passion, the stimulation of the skin where the pores of the skin are examined by hands, fingers, fingertips, lips, teeth and tongue. Sensitive spots will be exploited for future purposes. Warm oil shall be applied for a massage from head to toe. The reason for this is to say thank you. Thank you for entertaining me on those lonely nights. I would drown myself in you, the woman who I fantasize about, like melted chocolate all over your body. Are you touching yourself thinking about it? The chocolate is poured slowly so that you can caress it into your beautiful tattooed skin. My tongue will feel like a million tongues touching you at once; slowly cleansing your skin purposely and leaving chocolate causing several return trips. Imagine with all that heavy fucking I figured that maybe if you felt like some passion focused on just you!

MILF

I've always had an attraction to mature women, can't really say why, because I don't know why, I just do. For example Tina Turner had my ass shook watching her music videos. To me she was the world's sexiest grandmother, her legs and the way she presented herself; damn! But this ain't about her, it's about you as I've written prior all women have something that no other woman posses, but what was it about you that had me wondering.

JUST A FRIEND

I wanted to share something with you not because it would lead to sex but to show you that you are a woman if that's what you want/need to give you that boost/lift to get through whatever, then I offer myself to you for that task. What I may want/need is not of your concern; the focus is that you feel as you should . . . Like a Woman.

ORAL FACILITATOR

Come on now, stop playing. I have shit to do. Take a shower, after I'm done! Let's go now, is what I said. Because she still had that you full of shit look on her face. She took her panties off as I nakedly walked to the other side of her bed. My mind was locked to one thing, how many? Hold up; let me start from the beginning.

I walked into her bedroom fresh from the shower, body still damp from the baby oil. I looked down at her half asleep face and asked her how many she wanted. A look of confusion and curiosity was on her face as her head slightly rose from the pillow. I repeated it again, how many do you want? Still with the same look on her face, I just asked you how many nuts you want to bust when I eat that pussy? Oh you thought I was bullshitting this morning huh?

She replied seductively, one good one!! With that said, a moment when tongues attack begins! I slid under her sheets and comforter spreading her legs slowly as I locked in position she readjusted herself for maximum pillow comfort. The tip of my tongue touched the outer walls of her pussy. A very slight moan and twitch like a static shock passed through her body as I ran my tongue around her lips. Heavy breathing and deep sexy moans of pleasure were muffled by the sheets and comforter urged me to hear more. She was soaking wet, but that was just the beginning!

Sometimes I wonder about this thing that I have with the Oral Facilitation of Female Pleasure (I like eating pussy!) Eating pussy gets me mentally excited, knowing she busts as many nuts as she can, with only the use of my tongue! That is my thrill right there and don't get it fucked up the stroke is great but there is nothing like giving a woman as many screaming, cussing, and fussing nuts as she can stand!

As I said before my arms were locked in place! There was no escape from that one that she wanted!! My tongue ring was crossing her clit then the tip of my tongue; driving all her senses to frenzy!! I'm bald headed and like to use it. Don't you know? I used my bald head to stimulate her pussy and clit. Yes, I do! Rub my milk dud like head against her sweet pussy! Mmm, mmm, yes I did.

WHEN TONGUES ATTACK/ TWISTED

For those of you who do not know of this technique its name was just created . . . . Bald Headed Tongue-Fu. When a bald or large fore headed individual uses from chin to top of head to stimulate the pussy and clit please use caution when trying this, know your partner well before trying this for your own safety, to stimulate the clit and pussy unjustly to bring a nut that makes her body arch to escape the inevitable! Though the arched body makes her think she is safe until she realizes that I've moved right along with her. Brutal sounding isn't it? Her body tensed up to statue like form for five seconds, her breathing stopped, she was in her moment. Do you remember yours? I just bet you do.

THE WAY THEY FEEL

I must admit the Truth! Please don't judge me, I won't judge you! My goodness, the way that you ladies bodies feel to my touch in tights, fitting (not strangle) jeans, bare /hairy (let's not get crazy now!!?) legs, or stockings (you get the picture) stimulates my senses! My nerve endings in my fingers and palms tingle as they rub across the fabric. If I get the chance too, watch me as I touch the contours that accentuate you from waist down. My eyes will close to allow sight through my hands and fingers. The heat that emulates from those certain areas let me know exactly where I'm at without seeing where! Ladies you know exactly what I'm referring too, don't you?! I could go on and on about your cover or uncovered legs but for now consider this the beginning of . . . . , the way they feel!!!

THE WALK

She had that type of walk like she knew her pussy was Good! With each step she took her ass swayed with grace. Her thighs jiggled a little and flexed showing her muscles as did her calves. The fitting shorts she wore stopped right at that hook! That being, where her ass over laps the back of her thighs. Only a man whose mind is nasty would notice that little detail! An mine is such a mind to see that! Watching her walk too long would have you hypnotized! This chick had a brother dumbfounded staring at a vision of nastiness in motion! Damn she had that thing working! all I could do was enjoy the MMOMENT and imagine the FANTASY! That was some walk she had. Do you walk like that too?!

IT'S OEKTNG

See young woman, you ain't ready for this here ole man! I'm a put
something on you r young ass! Listen here, see you used to them young
boys an I'm an ole raisin. If you don't know, ask your mama! There
ain't no youthful fumblin' goin' on over here! I lick clits! Yes I said it
and I meant it, hold my tongue for know one! I don't have youthful
stamina no more. So I use my damn tongue. So young lady this here
ain't nothing tp play with! You better off calling ya mama for help and
as you would say, stay in your lane! Right?! Then you need to do that,
just to give you an idea about how I get down. When I'm through
licking your clit, there won't be nothing or no one that would make
you wet with thoughts of lust! From the memories of what I did to it,
think about it!!!!

MY OWN DOING

My dick was so hard it hurt last night an you were not available. I called and texted but you could not be reached. The thoughts of our last encounter flashed thru my mind. As well as the sensations of what we had done the night before. The thought, just the thought of what you tasted like caused my mouth to water. I swallow the lingering taste of your honey as though it were a drink! Remembering the way you caressed my body as though you were reading my thoughts. My skin reacts as though you've touched me but yet it's all in my mind! Even my own hands can not match the way you touched my flesh. From my bald head to my ankles and you know better than to be messing with my feet! My pierced nipple longs for your fingers, mouth and tongue to play with it! as well as the other sensitive spots you've found in your travels. Damn, my dick is so hard I can't think straight! An your ass ain't answering nothing! Now that's what I get for wearing your ass out like that, damn!!

I SAW YOU

You walked past me today as I was on my way to an appointment, I really didn't see your face but I was attracted anyway, for some reason a fantasy started. The hat that covered your short hair was the beginning because I like women with their hair like that. The clothes that you wore were casual, nothing that really would stop me in my tracks, however, as I searched for something more than that voluptuous ass of yours stood out. You did not seem to be slowing down so I could catch up to approach you, you walked with a purpose and thank you for that. All I could do was try to keep up and fantasize about the possibilities, wondering what it would be like to get you to the point of pure ecstasy, to be an everyday thought on your mind that stimulates you enough to make your pussy twitch with excitement.

YOU KNOW WHO YOU ARE

Damn, lil ma there is something about your pink lips that has me in a fantasy. That's the first thing I see when I see you, really it's true! I've got to look deeply into those sexy eyes because the thought of what those lips taste like overtake everything else. At times I allow myself to wonder what it would be like to see them cringe up from having a good climax or nut. That seems like it would be some really sexy shit. Then I get a lot nastier in my imagination and think if you're other lips look just as good! Then the thought of how many times you could cum crosses my mind too. As I write this I'm thinking about spinning your little ass around on my tongue. Damn, that mental visual has me excited, shit I need a moment my damn self!

FORTY ON UP

I've been called gay, I've been called a hoe, scary looking, beady eyed, bald headed, big nosed, fat, black, and ugly! Referred to as a door knob, every woman gets a turn. I was once mistaken as cute, can you believe that? My all time favorite is that I have a little dick. And the answer to that would be a yes! What did you really think I'd say, huh? I like the names for they fuel the fire that burns the pages of this book, with the imaginations of those that have, could, and maybe felt the natural flow of my mood! A mood of passion to please the mind, body, and spirit! This will touch your mind, stimulate your body and possibly fulfill your spirit. You will know when we meet I want to freak you! Rubbing my hand across my face fantasizing about you from your toes to the top of your head. Lusting after your body like an old man with a young heart! Mature women I see you but you rarely see me. One day you maybe able to see me on the internet. Am I too old for you? Do these young boys not know how to play these roles? Well slide on down this here side, mature, athletic cougars, confident in themselves enough not to fear any competition from younger ones. Those longing to be touched, held and fucked! The ole raisin is coming for you, to make you need that want satisfied and want that need satisfied as well!. Come find me if you dare, I won't tell, will you? I am waiting!

THINKING ABOUT YOU

Every time I close my eyes I wake up harder than understanding a woman! Do I now have your attention? I am talking to you woman, because not to many brothers are reading this here book! So honey I'm talking only to you. Remember when we caught eyes for that Moment? The smile and the how you doing. My eyes slyly take in your clothed body as we pass each other and yet you don't even realize that I'm stealing glances at you. Finding that thing makes me lust after you. Whatever it is, it carries my Fantasy of you to this paper for us to share. As black hueMAN's nasty imagination to make every single woman that reads this, to make herself cum! Let me know respectfully please, I want to know! My goal is to mentally TONGUE-FU you all! Imagine having your clitoris sucked while my tongue darted slowly in and out of your, you know! Wait! Don't touch it yet, stop! Also licking around your lips, all at the same time! I don't play or lie on this here. If my last friend with benefits ain't still upset, she will tell you. Stop touching your clit and stop rubbing your breasts! If you've got me audio please continue, shit, I'm writing this imagining you. Your voice, the moans, sighs and all that you could be saying. Really all I need to do is see you for my Moment to write about you! I'm comfortable in a place near you as I know this is the only thing filling my mind as I write. It's fucking with you isn't it? You see me don't you? My last friend with benefits was younger than me and of course she would refer to me as ole dude. Yet, I was not the one needing brakes and timeouts! Now bust that nut knowing what we share in this our Fantasy. On what verse do you bust on, huh?

GENTLEMEN'S CLUB HOPPING

Sister big bone come here let's dance. Strip for me baby please. If you do it right the TONGUE-FU will freely reward you! See I want to see you strip from fully clothed to thong, bra, stockings, footwear, and a smile. Oh how many fantasies you'll help create. Shake, gyrate, wiggle, bounce, pop, slow wind, clap, rock, and sweat! Baby if you do it right, oh have mercy if I bite my bottom lip off imagining you perform. My hands are shaking and its 3 am in the morning. This beat and chorus has me rocking on the edge of bed. Oh, oh sweet suga low and timbo! Start from the beginning after this and I'm going to close my eyes and imagine you dancing for me. Lean back and rub my dick through my Nike black shorts, and rub my chest, the right nipple mostly! Town to town I'm coming to see you! Do it!

STRIPPING FOR YOU TO A SONG

Girl, I'm cheating on my girl! Fucked up right? Yeah I know but listen to it a few times. Hear the story before you judge me. Now imagine me in front of you mouthing the words slowly taking my shirt off revealing a wife beater, somewhat defined tattooed chest and arms. Chinese eyes intriguing and mysterious, eyes that at times cause you to question if they are actually open or not. Pepper mint breath tickles that spot below your ear, sensations run down your spine to your tail bone. Your pussy starts to trickle too! Your knees buckle slightly causing a faint like movement. I am expressing the story that I wish that I could truly share with that one special woman, trying to be my friend. Imagine your own moment of hugs, kisses, and cuddles, foreplay for those who live as I, in the moment, flow with me as I cheat on you with you! The one and the same woman!

WHAT USED TO BE

Another Love TKO! Now what we used to do will be a Fantasy in many of my Moments. I hope they bring back what we shared when they flow through your mind, remembering the passion and what it felt like. The Moments when I was the need that you wanted fulfilled and the want that you needed to be fulfilled! Do you remember my flow? I once again thank you for what you've helped me achieve through our Moment together. The times when you blushed from my stares. Do you remember those stolen rubs hidden from the public eye? Lustfully groping you, making you feel desired when my body made you wet. My voice made you feel secure when you heard it, when I was Addictive! When you understood how I put on the hats of who you needed me to be at the time. The stolen Moments when the children were sleeping or outside. That freaky shit where you try your best not to scream! Begging me to let the TONGUE-FU lose from your clit or pussy! How my tongue would some how manage to hit your g-spot, still sucking your clit. The promise to always remain Friends through all the trials and tribulations, while flowing in our Fantasy Moments! I sometimes remember them and you. The angel that didn't belong to me, the cause of pain but I was fine. Also the role playing Fantasies that we shared. How we would cheat on each other with each other, keeping the intrigue of the roughneck, bear, beast black hueMAN! The stripping fantasies that I tried to perform for you! Do they flow through your mind sometimes? Anything you want, your own stripper, touch yourself as I tease and tickle the nasty wonders of your mind with a private show. Is your pussy wet remembering those Moments? The way you danced to music at parties as though no one was around, that flow that surrounds us as we perform acts of passion and lust on the crowded dance floor. Fully clothed forbidden dances that make all desire to share our flow! If you can feel my flow you see in your mind what I still hold in my Fantasies of what used to be! I know that old thing will not ever come back, when you fiend for me nightly. The beautiful nightmare and liar that was a guilty pleasure to you, denied at some point. You now read and wonder if I still want you. Well as you can read, as this track makes me wonder myself, if you now realize what we had. Yeah, I do at times still want you but the icebox that is my heart beats pure ice through my veins, I'm so cold! All thoughts and moves are calculated steps! We no longer talk and you've moved on. A new man occupies the space that I once held in your heart. I sometimes wonder why I can't let go of a hope that comes that we'd ever again truly be just friends! So as the music plays the love that's no longer shared, will wonder through my mind to play on stronger over and over! It must be nice having someone who'd walk the walk as well as talk the talk until then the oral facilitator of female pleasure, pro-lover on paper is now me! Loving mc baby is now a no, no! Flow with it, you still remember the beginnings don't you?

DISH CUSTOMER REP.

We just got off the phone and your name is echoing through my being, just the way you said it, hmm, the name drips from your lips. I read something to you that I had written earlier while out running errands. It went like this: I'll be around when you want me to come, call me! The Black hueMAN wears many hats, roughneck, bear, beast and the oral facilitator of female pleasure. I am described best by Usher's pro-lover, exactly the thing that you need to fulfill that want you need taken care of, no more, no less. Now listen to the song and imagine with me what we both look like to each other. It has begun, yeah NISHARE you are now part of my flow honey, slow wind with me baby! Sway to the beat spooning, cuddling, teasing, and lusting for me as I you from just that one Moment for this Fantasy. What those lips that let your name pass through them look like! Damn, NISHARE I want to hug you like only I could do. Where my strong tattooed arms wrap around you! Arms over my shoulders so that I can lift you off your feet, letting your back crack just from a hug. Looking deeply into sexy eyes that I can only imagine about. People have said that you could blind my ass with dental floss because they are so small. I consider myself to be fat and ugly with a little dick! But, a rare black hueMAN that likes to use his imagination! Imagine my bald head grinding against your pussy. Yes, my head just grinding pressing gently causing friction against clit and pussy at the same time. Your hands holding my head, rubbing,

36

caressing my milk dud. Your legs spread while your head's tilted back with your eyes and mouth open wide! Your thigh high stockings entice me more with the sight and feel of them, those stilettos are killing me. How did you know I like shit like that? Why don't you have panties on? Oh woman I like that about you! Adventurous, secure, and nasty! The way that skirt is hiked up, oh damn my dick is hard imagining all this Fantasy! From just once chance meeting you've put yourself in my Moments and Fantasies. If we meet . . . , now when we meet, they will get more detailed! For now just imagine the TONGUE-FU TEACHER who watches the Sons of Anarchy has just turned you out mentally. Don't be embarrassed, stop blushing. Hey don't peek under there! Imagine how I flow in spirit.

THE THINGS WE COULD DO

I remember you like it was yesterday. The anticipation of seeing you again fuels my lust for you. You are waiting patiently for my shower to end like a lioness prowling for her prey to appear. I appear with a towel draped around my waist with a bulge in front. Your eyes lust seductively at me as one finger slowly pulls down your bottom lip, while sitting up in the middle of the bed with a t-shirt and no panties on! Your nipples are peaking through the worn fabric yearning for my touch. Thick and juicy thighs and booty show slightly under the shirt. Your hair is sexy tapered in the back just the way I like it. As I approach the bed you start to lean back on your elbows and the graphic letters describing the way I would lick and suck on your body frightens you. Will it or won't it be like I wrote leaves your mind the second my tongue touches your big toe tracing and sucking it. Every manicured toe is individually caressed by my lips, pierced tongue, and teeth, and the foot is massaged at the same time. You take your shirt off exposing your firm breasts. The foot massage is now done and your feet feel like they are no longer there. The bearded clan's men approaches in order to munch the carpet, kiss the kitten, and suck the wet doughnut! You open your legs wide showing the view that makes me drool! My expression to the exquisite sight before me has you nervous now. Being good is not a concern anymore, it's whether or not you can handle coming, until I get tired. Don't worry I'll give you a break in between nuts. TONGUE-FU and the TWO FINGERS OF PLEASURE applied in ways not before felt. Tears of pleasure pour from the corners of your eyes. You've squirted for the first time, hands move from my bald head to breasts, to sheets, to your face; constantly reaching to brace yourself for wave after wave of orgasms of body rocking proportions, convulsing uncontrollably with hands covering your embarrassed face. I watch as I wonder what's going through your mind at this very second. What your does your body feel like right now? My mind imagines the wonders of that unthinkable description. I'm asking are you really ready? If so you deserve it!

PUT THIS TOGETHER

Feel me now! A CD I put together with various artists to create a mental orgasm. See if you can catch all the song titles to make your own feel me now CD to feel the natural flow of my mood. Spoken word, brother to the night is looking to be somebody's somebody! I am hoping you're my soul sista and angel to walk with me in the point of it all, the unthinkable. We could be going half on a baby until the break of dawn, if you were here tonight, beautiful. I yell there goes my baby to your reflection in the mirror because she's the chick I'm cheating on you with. She can sign your name at the same place at the same time in Shangeri-la. I'm fortunate to have someone see the best in me! Ask me somehow if you miss one, enjoy otherwise, my flow. This is only the beginning!

THE FRIEND WITH BENEFITS

I'm your sponsor all right that pro-lover, and oral facilitator of female pleasure. That ole raggedy teddy bear that always fulfills the need that you want to be fulfilled when that want needs to be fulfilled! The one you call when you just have to get a nut off, someone at times you've got to fend your clit off from. That's right ladies, I wrote it! There's no shame in telling the truth! When it's your time of the month he accurately attacks your clit only? Don't look surprised, I as do others still exist able to make you come from tossing your salad. What, that's never been done? Is he still not determined to make you come by sucking on your nipples? Close your mouth honey, it's all right in my mind. I see you baby!

LINGERIE FOOTBALL LEAGUE

Yeah ladies I'm looking at you all! You're all a part of my Moments and Fantasies, don't think your not! I'm Blessed with the ability to see your sexiness no matter what. My imagination gives that vision, so with that I share with you to always let you wonder if I'm writing about you. I am! Every one of you that I may come into contact with! As I write this the lingerie football league is playing as I write the lust that I have for these ladies playing football is vast! Oh hell yes pure uninhibited lust as a horny ole man as myself is. I still really love watching these women actually play. The Tampa Breeze versus the Baltimore Charm. Just so you know that I actually exist I'm watching and Fantasizing about many, many Moments!

SOMEONE DIFFERENT

I remember her mostly about how she had a different man for different needs and wants. One older, one younger, one gay, one with money, one married, and for sex, you get the picture. All these men fulfilled her needs and wants when they arose. I've often wondered about women and how many feel this way. I've tried to be all these men at once to find myself to still be single and wondering why. When none of them appreciated me or the black hueMAN that I was trying to be there for them, just a friend, a jack of all trades but a master of none. The pro-lover, oral facilitator of female pleasure, no more no less. I fulfilled the need that wants to be fulfilled and the want that needs to be fulfilled a friend.

SHE CROSSED MY PATH

From the pumps up is how I first saw you. Open toed sandals, hmm! The exotic tights fit your petite form so well, damn. They fit a little too well because the panty line showed! Wow, such an enticing view that had my mouth watering. Your juicy phat little booty flexed with every step calling for my absolute attention an got just that! The jacket you wore over your blouse covered very little of your exposed cleavage. Your eyes commanded a second look just to marvel at their beauty! I could see myself staring into them for hours, though their color escapes me. It really doesn't matter since they just add to the Fantasy. My imagination of the erotic things that I have in store for you are endless. Just the thought of gently caressing those tight covered legs up and down, teasing my hands as they touch your tights wishing it were skin. Caressing your covered booty with that hook that I like, you know where your cheek overlaps enough for my fingers to grip. Don't act like you don't know what I'm talking about because you do! I could see myself on my knees behind you licking you from the back. Spreading your cheeks so I can get to your pussy. Standing spread eagle up against a wall with that juicy little booty poked out! Damn, I'm getting hard imagining that right there. I'm so intrigued by your style that I really want you to keep your clothes on, that's right! Baby I want to get you hot and bothered until you start tearing your own clothes off! So let me rub that ass, squeeze a cheek and slide my fingers between and caress your pussy all through your tights! Getting you wet enough to soak through them as you slightly lose balance from the sensation of it all! As I reach from the front of you between your legs feeling just how wet I've gotten you! I lick my fingers, one at a time tasting the sweet juice that flows from you. So sweet! I could see you in two positions: one, back slightly arched and ass poked out and me face deep! Two, with your legs and pumps up and me face deep again! I would have shown you the positive affects that TONGUE-FU would give you. We were both in a rush so it seems there was no time to meet, but I remember those exotic tights!

MS. LDC

I arrived at her house not knowing what to expect. She only said that she had something special in place for me but didn't say what. We went straight into her bedroom where she undressed me totally, then led me to a bathroom full of candles and a hot bubble bath. Soft music played as she helped me get comfortable in the tub. The whole atmosphere was erotic and sensual but when her robe dropped to the floor, oh my, oh my! Even though I'd seen this woman naked before the setting made her even more attractive. The look on my face was that of a man with pure lust flowing through his veins. It only took her a few steps to get in the tub but that still took to long. When she sat on my lap in the tub the sensations of soapy skin enticed me further. Her back against my chest, head on my shoulder and my dick sitting right between her ass cheeks. My arms were wrapped around her as we sat in silence enjoying the Moment. Without words we looked into each others eyes and kissed deeply and passionately. Sudsy water washed down our bodies with each caress and touch. She spun around to face me with ease as bubbles and water slightly spilled out of the tub. Her hands rested on my chest as we kissed again, same as before. My hands caressed up and down her petite athletic body. The natural flow of my mood was in total passion mood. If you don't know what necking is go ask your mama. My mouth, tongue ring, teeth, lips, hands, fingertips all massaged above her waist. From what I did her pussy juice filled the tub even more adding to what overflowed from the tub. My hands didn't need to go below the bubbly water to achieve the goal. If you would like to know more about this Moment or possibly Fantasy holla at your friend, peace!

MR. MOM AND THEN SOME

You wake to the smell of breakfast cooking, still feeling the after effects from TONGUE-FU and the TWO FINGERS OF PLEASURE this morning. The children are up and handling their business, getting ready, lunches are packed as you all eat to start your day. We kiss seductively and playfully as you squeeze my ass heading out the door to work! The kids are dropped off at school and I return home. The dishes are cleaned and put away, the house is straightened up, laundry is done and the clothes are folded and put away. Since everything is finally done it is now time for me to work out, trying to keep it sexy for you. We playfully text throughout the day keeping it interesting! The children are at their grandparents now and you've just arrived home. I'm standing in the doorway in an apron totally naked underneath it. As I help you take your coat off I ask you one question. Dinner is cooked, now would you like dinner or would you rather be dinner? What would you chose?

THE BLACK WIDOW

The Fantasy started the Moment that she stepped out her front door. My stare was like a beast stalking its prey. I got out to open her door, no chivalry is not dead, and the Fantasy got hotter! She approached the open door with a seductive, intriguing confidence, hair pulled back, face slightly kissed with make-up, and blouse revealing voluptuous cleavage, slightly fitted denim skirt with black fish net stockings and black leather stiletto knee boots. Damn, that motherfucka was sexy as hell walking towards me. An damn, my mouth is watering as I write this shit right now, damn! We exchanged greetings and hugs before she got in. Mmm, she smelled and felt so good between my arms. With hesitation I let her go and helped her in the truck. As she raised her thick sexy ass leg to get in I thought I was going to lose my mind. Oh my goodness! Her skirt was slightly fitted but tight enough to have to be pulled up a little bit to get in! As I write and see this image in my mind, mmm, mmm. She didn't know how she had me twisted right there but if she had asked, boy I would have slid my tongue way deep into her pussy! Nasty ain't I? She slid that juicy booty into that seat and my mouth got jealous! I paused for a second to take in the view of her sitting there before I shut the door. As I walked to the driver's side my imagination took over and from there, and well . . . , if this ever published ask for a more in depth view into this Fantasy and Moment!

HALF TIME

Thank you baby for letting me watch the game uninterrupted! Thank you for the food and drinks you made and served to me. The fact that you actually sat down with me and tried and I do mean tried even through me yelling and screaming at the TV you understood a little. That right there, boy they don't make 'em like you too often! Now just before the second half ends I need you to do something for me, go lie on the bed and get ready. For what you ask. Half time baby, half time! Let me explain real quick. Half time lasts for twenty minutes which means I'm going to find out how many times I can make you cum! Okay smile and walk please because half times about to start and you are still looking at me like I said some shocking shit! Take that ass on now. Go pee or whatever, wipe, and wash off, whatever the hell you going to do just keep moving while you're grinning your ass off. Damn! Don't mess up the flow baby, cause when half time starts I go pee and then I eat you! You should and will be semi naked or fully naked it really does not matter to me as long as I can look and see every single inch of your sweet ass pussy in view. Don't touch it, don't rub it, just leave it alone! The only thing that's going to touch it is my tongue, tongue ring, teeth, lips, mustache, chin piercing, and goatee; my hands won't even touch it! Yeah, I'm really like that, just down right nasty! My arms will be locked in until half time ends, so be prepared! I like that you've done what I have asked. Damn, how good you look laying there, like bacon, egg sandwich. Shit, I had to lick my damn lips thinking about how good you'd taste while I'm writing this, hope you are too! I'm thinking about you to, whatever woman is reading this! Too late, I'm locked in just as "Fortunate" plays from the Feel ME Now CD I made. Deeply breathing my hot altoid scented breath closely to your pussy teasing, yes, I know and time is of the essence.

I start licking and sucking your lips like it was your mouth, passionately! Your body tenses up, hands grab the sheets as I continue my kisses, your moans try desperately to escape your throat. The moans stop as I address your clit with the same passion. You cum with force within what seems like seconds and you push or try to push me back, like I said try! Your hands give in and grab your breasts, squeezing them tight and trying to hold back that next nut that's quickly approaching! You still can't understand how my tongue does that to you as it crashes into your body like a heavy weight. Meanwhile your butt is pushing hard into the bed trying to escape my tongue! I cut you a break, oh I didn't unlock my arms and now I'm just breathing on your pussy, heavily! By the way I'm counting to ten, yeah ten seconds. What? I counted slow! Now I'm licking around your clit especially the hood setting you up for the Tongue-Fu, the art of sucking your clit while licking in and around your pussy walls and hole. Damn, I'm getting hard, shit I need to lick you right now! Tongue-Fu has your eyes closed shut, shoulders are pressed firmly to the mattress and your mouth is wide open ready to scream, while your legs are pushing upward too. Yet they are failing because of the vise like grip I have on them. My mouth is locked on your clit, my tongue ring is circling and darting in and out of you. Suddenly you loosen up completely and melt into the bed with your mouth open and your eyes stare blankly into space. Before your ass can hit the mattress you tense up again, this time somehow you shoot out of my arms, briefly! Halftime ain't ended yet baby! Tongue-Fu has caused you to now beg and plead between breaths and moans, now ma-fucka! I told you I was hungry and half time is twenty minutes and it hasn't been ten minutes yet! I ease back a little and start back to kissing your lips as you slowly come down from that furniture moving nut and you start to rub my bald head. Then it starts to rub on your clit, pussy lips, and hole! Well, I said I was nasty before so what's the matter? I'm nasty tested and approved! Up and down, slowly, gently pushing a little to give that feeling of pressure, twisting and turning my bald head all over your pussy and clit. Ever so often I put the crown of my head to the bottom of your pussy, rolling my head up so my forehead crosses your pussy, spreading your lips down between my eyebrows to my pierced nose, across my mustache, past my upper lip to my flattened tongue and gently brushing the hairs of chin. This gets you back to where I can squeeze a few more nuts out of you before the game starts again! Now you're like baby the game's about to start again? I know was all I said before sucking your clit into my mouth again.

Oh shit baby is all I heard before her legs started to shake. She grabs her breasts and pinch her nipples tight. Her pelvis rocks up and down as I suck and lick at the same time. Before long she comes again and this time she squirts too! Somehow she wiggled out of my grasp to hop off the damn bed with her hands on her hips rocking back and forth trying to catch her breath. She managed to say, halftimes over, and go wipe your face. But just as she was saying that I was already licking her sweet honey from my chin piercing and goatee. With a sly look as I walked out the room I said we'll pick this up after the game. That's what my halftime Moments are like. How about yours?

Mmm, look at you working out! I just happened to glance over and notice you looking oh so sexy jogging through the park. Damn, just look at you! Your hair is in a ponytail, sports bra underneath your tightly fitted shirt. Tights cover your thongs that peeks out with each stride. Your calves are exposed, sexy and strong flexing and relaxing with every step, ankle socks and sneakers complete your sexy work-out attire. I know you have your weight goals that you're trying to reach, but damn honey as far as I'm concerned you don't need to lose too much. The way your booty cheeks individually flex and bounce is enticing. Your thigh muscles show and ripple, succulent breasts heave up and down, mmm! Please don't lose too much because only dogs like bones! You have to be able to provide shade when it's sunny and warmth in the winter. Watching you has me imagining about a Fantasy starring you. I know after a work out you are going to want to jump in the shower and that would be the normal thing to do but not today. Today after you work out I'm going to work you out! I'll have a towel waiting for you to wipe the perspiration from your forehead and face. Then I will tongue you down with more lust than passion because now I'm beyond turned on!

DO YOU REALLY WANNA?!

Do you really think that you can handle this? This is one thing that all who has met me knows this is to be true. I am unlike any other man that you've ever met. I have no problem making you feel like Halle, in Monster's Ball or remaking the scene from Purple Rain. Your outer body will have an outer body experience! No matter the man after me, you will always fantasize about the things I do to you. Flashes will make you horny and wet, of my hooped tongue and the unknown before heights it brought you. I did say hooped tongue, that's for a purpose not for show! The way my strong hands massaged, caressed, and teased your entire body the oral facilitator of female pleasure is a devoted pussy eater. Now, do you think you can act like you don't know me when it's through? I can because I've learned to accept things for what they are, a M & F in both of our lives, so do you really wanna . . . ?

MORNING BREATH

I just opened my eyes and tasted the little bit of saliva in my mouth. After giving thanks for my awakening and having what I think is a sound, mind, and body; the taste in my mouth demands my attention. What flavor is this that's stimulating my senses? Then you sigh and instantly the taste is known. It's you! The taste of your sweet nectar has me aroused. The fact that you have no panties on has my mouth watering! I feel faint seeing that you've slept face down, ass up! And now I not only know what but also the why and the how. Let me ask you this, what do you think I am about to do in this situation at this time? Do I a: get up and brush my teeth and risk waking you up without making this M & F real? Aww, hell no! Or do I b: spread them ass cheeks wide and give her a damn thrill she won't ever forget? Aww, hell yes! Now if I have to wait for you to figure this out, please have yourself checked. I have not come across too many women who sleep ass up. It isn't like your (she's) going to mind once that hoop crosses that clitoris and ass. At first it's all going to seem like a dream to her until she explodes, sending her to the land beyond, beyond. I'm going to wake that ass up and knock it back out at the same time. Then she better hope that I don't slam some dick, balls deep into her juicy coochie. Oops, did I just write that? That's another story right there! The weight of my upper body will hold her down while she travels to that land. And that is the reason for my morning breath! Ain't I nasty!

INSIGHT

I wrote this with no ego, pride or any type of macho B.S. in my heart nor my mind. It was written to let all the women of the world know that I think about you even though we may not ever meet. You will understand and relate to my flow. Through it you will feel as though we have met before. As I walk this earth I see each of you ladies for the gifts that you are; such visions of beauty to behold everyday that I'm awakened to see. At your worse or best I can still see a M & F that we could share. There will be more entries to come, so somewhere you will find that I'm writing about you. Yes, you holding this book! I want what you're reading to make you hot, bothered and wet. A friend of mine told me that after reading some of these M & F's she wanted/needed some dick and only the real thing would do! No it was not mine she was referring too. It didn't bother me at all, just the fact that it affected her that way, and with a sly smirk on my face, I hope it does the same to you! The song "Fifty Candles" by Boyz II Men just floated into my head. Can you feel my flow now? Come deeper into my flow if you dare. I sometimes write the titles of songs that I flow too at times. If you catch them make yourself an MP3 or CD and hear the natural flow of my mood! Listen, understand and relate to a man unlike any other man that you've met in your life. If ever by chance we share a physical M & F know this, protection is a requirement!

My friends are people that help without question when possible. Do not sugar coat the truth, listen all times and not just sometimes. They try to understand so that we can relate in someway. My friends know that not only do I love them as I love myself; they also know that I actually like them as people. Whatever it is that you may want please ask me. Remember this though, friend first! I have been called many things for many reasons, but understand this, I am a clitologist! That's what makes my dick hard. This hooped pierced tongue all over that button as you experience the joy it brings until you can't take it any more. Ole Eddie Kane, the Next Generation; remember the name!

OVERLY EXCITED

She was on my mind all day! What I wanted to do was leave an unforgettable impression. The supplement I took for reassurance had my body hot. Upon arrival there was no kiss or foreplay, which is a turn off but I was willing to adjust. Just how fat and round her booty was motivation enough for some; for me I wanted more than just her body. I wanted her mind like she expressed that I had. With her booty in full view, the beast in me came out. I stroked her from behind like it was my last! She arched her back so that she could see my face between strokes, which were forceful going in and slow coming out. The way her booty shook with every pump sent chills down my spine! This was an M & F within itself. The feelings that friction causes displayed on our faces, changing with every stroke. Some expressions were funny and we both laughed without losing pace. Others made me almost lose my composure too soon! A brother had to make the necessary adjustments to keep that from happening just yet. She understood the game and knew to adjust also!

I had to stop looking at her expressions because they were causing too many close calls. The sounds she made changed with every orgasm she had. They seemed to build in force with each one; so I changed the variation of hand grabs with them all. My hands would hold her hips, pulling her back to meet my thrusts, squeezing her breasts and nipples at times switching hands and pressures applied. At times seductively biting or massaging her shoulders and licking between her shoulder blades, leaning on her back as I let my fingers play with her coochie lips and clitoris, as I continue to stroke. There were times when one hand and fingers tickled her clitoris as the other pinched her nipple. I lost track of how many times she came but I knew she was enjoying what I was doing. Her coochie started releasing (farting) with my every thrust and her legs started to tremble as sweat and juices were running down her thighs. Her face could no longer be seen since it was buried deep in the pillow that she clutched tightly. Suddenly she looked back at me as if to say what are you doing back there? The she shot forwarded off me with her body shaking and gyrating. I could see her coochie pulsating and releasing air (farting) and that plump juicy fat booty is all exposed in the air took me to an M & F by itself. Then reality hit . . . the supplements had me so hot that I was not able to perform. I could only wonder about the possibilities! An overly excited first impression, not good.

FREAK'EM DRESS

She had planned her night out with the girls for awhile; everything was in order for her, just the girls and a night out on the town. The chorus to Fancy by Drake played over and over as she got ready, paying extra attention to every detail of herself from head to toe. The long bubble bath to exfoliate her skin, to the facial she gave herself. Her feet and finger nails were professionally done as was her hair. She caressed her body as she applied lotion to her curves and contours. At times she had to catch herself before she got too stimulated by her own touch. She admired herself as she put on her matching thong and bra set with thigh high stockings in her mirror. The dress she picked out was a freak'em special. It fit just right and teased the eyes with every move. The stiletto boots completed the look that she had wanted to achieve. Eye liner and lip gloss were the only things left to take care of. When she was finished she stood in the mirror smiling at herself thinking, I am one sexy bitch! There was a swagger that could not be missed as she walked into the room that I was in. Her walk was already sexy but this time it was more noticeable. The perfume that she wore tickled my senses as she strutted by me. I watched her like a lion eyeing his prey, readying to pounce. She was oblivious to my stares and forgot how I am when she's dressed in a freak'em dress as she left the room. The horny little man inside me thought she must really think she's going to make it out of here with that on! Just then she came back through, before she knew what hit her she was on the couch with one leg hanging over my back and the other just touching the floor, the freak'em dress was up around her waist, hands bracing her weight on the cushions. Her eyes were rolled up in her head like the exorcist or something. Her glossed lips shaped to make ooh ahh sounds from deep inside of her. My left hand has pulled the thong to the side exposing her clitoris that I had in my mouth. My tongue ring and tongue were delightfully assaulting it to a mind blowing orgasm. Yeah she's going out this house tonight floating on air but she's getting a hard nut before she goes out. The only thing twisted will be her head, her clothes; her makeup and hair will be untouched. I say twisted because after that orgasm, climax, nut or whatever you call it, she's still trying to figure out how she got in this position! At one point she was about to go out and hang with her girls and now she's about to have an outer body experience. The build up is more than she thought, she can now see herself just before she reached her point. Abruptly I stop my assault on her clitoris and I stand wiping her juices from my face with my hand and licking my fingers. She has a look of disbelief and shock on her face when I say now enjoy your evening with your girls and when you get back I'll finish the job; while sitting down and turning the TV on as I speak. That is what happens when you put your freak'em dress on around me! You were warned!

THE LOOK

It is something about the way that she looks at me every time we see each other. I think it may just be me reading too much into it but, hmm the possibilities, boy does my nasty little mind wonder about them all. The start, the middle, and the finish! I'm telling you I would do everything to make that one Moment feel like her never ending Fantasy mine would start the Moment that we were alone together. She would have an understanding of the natural flow of my mood and be a very willing participant. The only thing that would be surprising to her is how in-tuned I would be with her mind and body. That feeling of euphoria where only her pleasure was the focus of my passion and pleasure. Where she felt that no other person exists or mattered at that time to give you another mental picture, watch the scene in the movie Purple Rain, where their clothes stayed on; yeah, some real old school nasty stuff. Are you feeling me now?

MY OUTLOOK

Lay with me and let your mind see through my eyes a Moment and Fantasy! You may not see me but you will feel me. I am truly in touch with myself on all levels, so don't knock it until you've tried it only applied to certain things. Now I have not ever been attracted to anything that looks like me. No offense to anyone that is just me, but if you imagine what I've written using your on characters, be my guest. I will not be offended in any way as long as you enjoy reading it. Hopefully this will be an ongoing series that I share with you. Journeys into the mind of the Oral Facilitator of Female Pleasure, Ole Eddie Kane The Next Generation, meet me on the moon, find out what she meant.

JUST ONE KISS

You look so sexy that I just want to kiss you, embrace you in passion while deeply kissing your pretty lips, while ever so often gazing deeply into your eyes. They take me deeper into the untamed, unbridled, relentless desire that I have for you right now. Our lips and tongues dance to music that only we share saliva and the peach wine add to the intensity of the kiss. Arms tightened around each other slightly constricting air. Inhales and exhales damn near match breath for breath. Firm hands rub deeply as if giving one another simultaneous massages, at times I hold you too tight but I just can't seem to get close enough. I'm hard as a brick and your soaking wet yet there's barely any friction between the two of us. Your lips are so succulent and they're so full and juicy; I call them "ooohh" because every time I see them I make that face. A kiss from you is like Lay's Potato Chips, you can't just have one!

THAT SKIRT

I saw her and wasn't fazed at all initially for she was just an average woman. Then she stood up and all that changed! All of a sudden a Fantasy began in just that Moment. A hand shake and a smile is how she greeted me, very professional. Even though I was there being taken care of she paid attention to my words. She made quick work of a phone call to hear me speak. I didn't really notice the open toes neither sandals she wore nor her blouse. But what intrigued me the most was that skirt! It was a denim skirt but nothing to fancy. The way that she wore it had me horny! My nasty mind was working in overdrive. She didn't bend over, wiggle or anything out of the ordinary. Yet the thought of her right leg hanging over her desk, the left over my shoulder. My left index finger pulling her thong to the side, with my right hand holding her left thigh. Her arms holding her up to see my hoop pierced tongue approaching her clitoris. My hot breath has sent shock waves through her inner thigh. The thought of seeing her skirt pushed up because I've spread her legs wide, has me even more aroused. Drool forms on my tongue; the ever insatiable desire for pussy juice has the Oral Facilitator of Female Pleasure thirsty! What I'm about to do to this little woman her will make her rethink a lot about her outlook on life! Don't look shocked, please cover your mouth Boo—Boo! Yeah I can see/feel your reaction to this. No matter what she had before me or what she is used too when the two fingers of pleasure and tongue—fu hits that ass everything will shift. The anticipation as her eyes focused on my forth coming tongue and lips. Her senses deceive her as to the distance of my mouth with the heat of my breath. Her mouth is open wide ready to form sounds of lust, desire, and passion. For some strange reason she knows without reason that her pleasure will be fulfilled more than she could ever imagine. I'm so horny writing this right now that I could wave to you without using my hand. Remember you want the truth, right? Well here it is and so now deal with it! When all is said and done she will use what I've done to her as a guideline for her future endeavors. If we should ever share this Fantasy it would live up to the expectations. Until then it will be a Moment that I share with you through this that you read. All this from a skirt! Imagine what else would spark an M & F!

RAIN MAKER

I called her rain maker because every time we kissed the song, "Making Love in the Rain" by Herb Albert would play in our ears! Talk about truly feeling my flow! Even if our clothes stayed on it was still nasty and passionate. Her satisfaction is achieved through her clothes into her panties (even better down her thigh). Trust me on this one; she brought an extra pair of panties (or a towel or both). Her rain poured down like a flash flood; I knew she was capable but she didn't know her warning signs. For some reason it always seemed to rain whenever we were together. The way our eyes would speak to one another in our own language. The way the rain made our skin feel as we embraced. She as many others have longed for my back cracking hugs. Her feet dangle as she let's go into my strong arms. The release of pressure on her spine has her feeling faint. The rain that caresses her face keeps her conscience. Her wet hair attracts me more to her. Looking deeply into each others eyes as the rain drops fall between us our kiss is one that causes only the sounds around us to matter in this M & F that we'll share if ever we meet, until then I imagine you my . . . ,!

WHAT I WANT YOU TO DO

A disclaimer needs to be filed on this one right here. Ready? This is how I want you to suck my penis, cock (don't sound right), Johnson, prick, schlong, one eyed trouser snake, whatever name you want to give it, dick! These will be very simple instructions for you to follow. Please read it slowly or twice if you are in disbelief in what you will have read! I'll begin with the don'ts: Don't bite, scratch or skave it with your teeth! Don't wring it like it's a wash cloth or rag. Don't pinch it either! These don'ts also apply to my testicles, gonads, marbles, huevos, jewels, balls. You can even take it out my pants or shorts depending on the situation. Please make sure that the elastic or zipper is away from my balls before you begin. Begin you wonder? Yes, begin to caress it with your fingers, hands, and palms. Stroke it slowly up and down while paying attention to my reactions. Tease my scrotum sack with the tips of your fingers. You will start to notice that it will start to grow in width and length. It won't grow to big so don't get your hopes up! Take your lips and tongue and kiss, lick all around the head. While you're doing that, stroke it up and down slowly. Unless you have small hands use both of them if not only one is required. With your free hand you can either caress or cup my balls or rub my chest. By this time I will be harder than Chinese arithmetic. Now whatever techniques or tricks that you may know feel free to use them at your discretion. Act like it holds the cure to all things that ail you and the only way to get it out is by mouth. You can use that and your hands nothing else! Will you stand up to the challenge? I know I will be like I am now! The sounds that you make excite me even more, however you act is how I react.

FEMALE RADIO PERSONALITY

The topic of someone's past was the question that connected me to you. In a round about way I let you know that your past is not a factor in what could be our future. You felt that whatever your past was you wouldn't be judged if it was told to me! Why should it? Whatever you did then has no bearing on what we're trying to do now. If it does give me a heads up on that before we get started, that shows me a little about who you are as a person. I'm already attracted to your voice but then I just so happened to come across a picture of you! Lawd, have mercy! Just when I thought that I couldn't get any uglier than I already am! You are a very attractive woman from the picture I saw and the brief chat that we had before. I would like to get to know you as a person if possible one day but for now I am going to let my nasty mind imagine a while just from the photo. I enjoy the view of a woman in a short dress and heels. Tell me are your thighs as strong as they look? I should have kept the photo but my memory has not failed me so far. The way that your thigh showed through the fabric was stunning in itself! The wonder of having them wrapped around my head is taking me deeper into this M & F! I couldn't help but imagine my hand where yours were. What would that feel like to pull you to me by your hips? To look deep into your eyes and be lost in them. Your lips would peak my interest as to what they would feel and taste like! I'm getting a little bothered right now with that thought. Question, can you kiss and would you consider yourself a good one? I ask because the art of foreplay or old school necking is a thing of the past. The build up to the actual act gives me an idea of what you'd like and dislike. What would get you to think hard about me until the time was right. Just in case that day ever comes when we re-visit our Moment and Fantasy it shall be written in my M & F.

ARE YOU HER?

I know what you like and what you want. She wants that old thing back! She likes that hooped tongue that's phat. I know she thinks about it and every time she does she gets horny and wet. Another lover with a great tongue game still wouldn't satisfy her. Whatever it is that I possess keeps her desiring me; forever will she deny it but her body language and actions say otherwise. Gone are the nights when she was awoken by the piercing to her booty. When the dream became a reality and then a thought that always lingers, a beautiful reoccurring nightmare! She could not shake the memories of so many times to be awaken in such a manner, at times the memories would cause her pussy to get juicy! Her hands would subconsciously travel to her clit and nipples to caress those areas; whether they are clothed or unclothed. She has to catch herself at times lost in the Moment and Fantasy that now is a memory. The description of how she felt from inner skin friction, no matter whom, the results still do not compare to what I used to do to her. It always seems to escape her when it comes to figuring out what was it that I had done to her. Forever more will her body and mind long for the attention women would only dream of. Now she can only fantasize of a real M & F that has passed. Her pride keeps her from the need that she wants to be fulfilled and the want that she needs fulfilling! She denies not only herself but me as well! What a selfish heffa she is!

THIS CHICK

She made the comment of it better be good. Oh, really, did she just challenge me, the Oral Facilitator of Female Pleasure? That's what it sounded like to me. The real question is: are you sure you want to hang with Ole Eddie Kane, the Next Generation? I had to give her the benefit of the doubt because she could not imagine what I was going to do to her. Our attraction to one another would be of a pure curiosity, finding out what the other was capable of doing to the other! Well, she was about to get her clit licked better than two lesbians at once! And yes it is like that! Only thing is my dick hardens the more I pleasure her. The clothes that she arrives in will only excite and arouse me even more. Her fear of the unfamiliar will fade quickly as I relax her mind. The alcohol she sipped seemed to build her confidence. That second hug she requested was more than I expected. The seductive and sensual way that she wrapped her legs around my waist from start to finish was like a human python. Damn, I'm getting excited my damn self! I can feel her breath on my neck as my scent stimulated her coochie to twitch. After a deep breath she faces me with her eyes closed. The way she opened her eyes slowly as her head turned slightly to kiss me passionately. Our peppermint scented breath mixes, sending chills down our spines. The piercing in our tongues clink together as they explore new territory. Music plays in the background intensifying the kiss even more. She grinds her body into me as she slides down until her feet touch the floor. The look in her eyes after her breasts get pushed up by the bulge she created and the way she rubbed her lips and body let me know that she was excited about the possibilities of what's about to happen! If she could have read my mind or expression on my face she would have known for sure I was about to make her see herself having an orgasm every time she opened her eyes just before it hits! This would be her first experience with the creator of the Tongue-Fu and the Two Fingers of Pleasure that would linger in her memories for life. They say you always remember your first, right? Many will try but no one will achieve giving her the same feeling! Now if she has multiple orgasms let's see if she will or can tap out. Try not to lose count okay? No words were spoken as she sat down on the couch and before she knew what had happened my tongue was lapping at her wet thong. One leg was over my shoulder and the other was bent pointed in another direction. Her sweetness is spilling out the sides of her thong as I continue to lick her every drop. Her facial expressions changed often from the friction of texture and hoop on my tongue. Unable to fight the force she busts her first nut and I haven't even touched her clit yet. Oh, sister is in trouble and now she knows it! The teacher is in, class is now in session. Before her first break she has to bust at least three more after this first one. Her thong is stretched over her clit and love tunnel. She's breathing very hard like somebody was choking her ass with each stroke of my tongue.

What she was used to is no longer satisfactory to her. The mind and body must flow like the yin and yang as one! This feeling is addictive like nicotine without the side effects. As I French kiss her lips without teeth she rubs my bald head with both her hands and fingers. She touched herself as she tries to stimulate herself the way my tongue does when I teasingly stop at times. This one time I stop to take a mental picture of how beautiful her partially exposed body looked. It was a quick glimpse before she grabbed the back of my head and pushed my face back to her coochie. The combination of hoop and tongue twisted her ass right up! When my tongue slide into her tunnel she tensed up until she adjusted to the sensation I was giving her. Those perky breasts of hers were squeezed together tightly like her eyes with both hands on either side of my head. She was mouthing something but no words came out. Then in a nasty and horny voice she yells, "I'm coming again. Oh, shit!" That's when I applied the Two Fingers of Pleasure; that would be an index finger in her coochie, the middle in her ass. I wish I could have recorded her reaction so that I could watch it over again! She shouted oh so very seductively, "Oh, shit I'm still coming!" Her hands gripped tightly to her breasts, feet planted firmly in the cushions as her legs shook and trembled. The look on her face was the need she wanted fulfilled and the want that she needed to be filled. I was excited even more just by her expressions as they passed through her. She had a tight grip on my fingers until she was able to adjust to the sensations they were giving her. Then slowly she rolled her hips in a circle making her coochie and ass swallow my fingers with each circle more of my fingers went into her until my thumb was rubbing her clit. Moans of pure ecstasy from deep down in her diaphragm let me know she wanted/desired more. I teased her clit with the tip of my tongue and thumb as I enjoyed her enjoyment. That Moment was very brief for her when Tongue-Fu locked on to her clit. Tongue-Fu is the sucking of a clit while licking the lips and sliding in and out of her honey pot. Plus, the Two Fingers of Pleasure are also included in the action. This chick did not know who she was fucking with! The look on her face was that of lustful anger, like damn where the hell have you been! I could feel her trying to hold back the orgasm that was coming by the way her hips sunk into the couch. Her breath was slow and deep, her arms above her head bracing for the nut. The suction that was on her clit got a little tighter as I wiggled both my fingers inside her, with Tongue-Fu and the Two Fingers together she didn't hold back long! I could feel her little fingers on the back of my head just before she came! "I'm about to, oh shit" were the words I heard as she exploded unexpectedly and squirted while she was grinding on my face! Surprised, she let my head go only for me to adjust for the next squirt. It came just as the hoop on my tongue flicked her clit. It seemed as if someone had turned a faucet on as her juices flowed and she oohed and ahhed, and tapped out on the cushion. I looked at her beautiful and spent body as I slowly eased the two fingers out of her. The more I admired my handy work, as she squeezed her breasts together trying to regain her composure, the sexier she became. When she opened her eyes she looked directly at me and in between deep breaths she managed to say, "That was the first time that happened." I'm standing there thinking to myself this chick forgot that I brought dick too!

ACT RIGHT

Excuse me miss, could I have just a moment of your time? Just a moment. Hopefully I'm not keeping you from anything important. Please let me know and hopefully if not we can talk for a while, if you do then maybe another time. I don't mean to offend you but there's something about you that makes me want to cheat with you girl, if you was my girl! Miss Independent (I love you because she got your own) are you my soul sista. Or the angel that makes me believe we could do the unthinkable. Could you be my somebody's somebody? An have me thinking about going half on a baby. Hey no disrespect just being truthful about mine! The need that you want fulfilled, the want that you need fulfilled. The sweet dream beautiful nightmare, the thought you feel in your body when I cross your mind. Who I am is whoever you want me to be. But if a name is what you require, just call me Act Right! The thing you need to help or get you too, Act right!

HER NAME WAS?

The first time I saw her, she was all I saw. She was beautiful! Her skin was flawless brown as were her eyes, hair a style that fit her to a tee, athletic frame, medium in height and damn written all over. Just her eyes had me intrigued, soft yet piercing like she saw something she wanted and was locked in. She knew what she liked and didn't hesitate to let you know what it was. One lazy mid morning I woke up to see her beautiful face and got lost in a moment. A moment where nothing else exists just me and her. It was just warm enough to not have a sheet cover her naked body; my thoughts were of how beautiful this woman was laying before me. Desire, lust, and passion surged inside of me. The more I looked at her the more I wanted to mmm, it's hard to explain, I had to be one with her. I wanted her to feel all that I felt at the MOMENT. She awoke with my tongue bathing her body from toes to finger tips. Nothing was missed but I lie, her clitoris. I know how much she loved the way I licked her clitoris. To me that was what I'm here after if you believe in the here and after! The oral facilitator of clitoral pleasure. Yeah, I like to EAT PUSSY! A Black Man that likes, correction loves to! There is no youthful fumbling either!

I'm going right for the button. She tasted so good, her juices flowed and I tried my damnedest not to miss a drop. She came with such a force but I couldn't stop pushing her button. After her second orgasm I enter her as she spreads her legs so that they rest on my arms. The deeper I went the better it felt for both of us. I moaned her name, tight eyed, slowly stroking back and forth, words of pleasure passed our lips between passionate (deep) kisses and moans, touches and caresses played across our bodies. She came again, flipped over on her stomach and oh my goodness! My eyes have closed and my head is turning left to right thinking about that right there, man that sent a shock through me! Sorry I had a moment just thinking about what I saw. A woman on her stomach . . . , guys knows what I'm talking about! If she could've seen the look on my face but she already knew the look of a man whose only desires to please her. I devoured her asshole, licking and flicking all to hear her moan. Top to the bottom, her bottom to her top, clit to booty, booty to clit, my saliva mixed with all her juices enticed me more. I filled her pussy to the brim as my, hands gripped strongly around her waist! I held her there for a MOMENT enjoying how it felt once again and then this muthafucka eased up and wham! She threw my ass off! Not literally, but when that pretty round muscular ass hit back! Damn she rocked me back enough that my man came out to the head. Now see that's what got her fucked up, not only did I return the favor I made sure she pleaded for a break. Her break was from the time my tongue hit that button while she sat on my face; (Oh yeah, I'm a nasty one, yes I is!) until she busted again! Hit my ass daddy! MMM it don't get no better than this (oh yes it does). We've been here before but I had all intentions of taking her to heights not reached before. She moaned and growled with pleasure at the same time, taking all I had to offer. I remember her telling me how she enjoyed the pleasure and pain of what we were doing that made her more desirable than ever. I could see all the expressions of lust, pain, ecstasy, and pure primal passion wash through her body! Her beautiful face didn't lose its beauty though it was distorted and contorted. Steady paced stroking in and out of her tight ass had me in a trance. My mind was thanking the Creator for this moment. Our moans and cries of pleasure and pain lightly echoed through the room. The windows were open but barely a draft of cool air passed through them. The outside world was moving but nothing mattered or was cared about! Her forbidden zone was explored for what seemed like hours from doggie to missionary to sideways to cowgirl and reverse cowgirl. Not that I didn't enjoy every stroke but I LOVE PUSSY! I'd jump over a forbidden zone and a blow job for a pussy.

IT'S THE EYES

I walked in an saw those eyes so seductive that they were scary! That eye to eye contact had me Fantasizing about climbing up under that desk an giving her a foot and leg rubbing! That would make her think that she was coming! What, did you think I was going to say, Nasty?! What, you thought I might have said something like, I'd be giving her clitoris a oral massage with my tongue?! Yeah, it did cross my mind! Got my mouth all watering for some, hold up, hold up! I don't know her like that! No offense, boo but me no know you that well! So the foot massage that I would give her would have her wondering. If he's this good with his hands then what is he with his hooped tongue?! Your toes would be attended to individually so that each would be equally tended too. The soles of your feet would be kneaded, rubbed and caressed. Heels and ankles stretched and loosened up with strong hands covered with massaging oil. Then I start rubbing her calves slowly, firmly giving them the attention that's long overdue. She's sitting in her high chair trying to keep her composure as the customers think it's her usual self. Her facial expressions change before them and her words are deeper and slower when spoken. I peek up from time to time to see her facial expressions which turn me on even more. She went from perspiring to sweating real, quick when I started on her thighs! I could really say it was a wrap when my hands touched right above her knee. The heat that was generating from between her thighs was intense. I knew she was wet by the way the cushion felted when my hands touched it. The scent of her flower was intoxicating, leaving me to desire a taste of her essence! Mmm, mmm, mmm, just the thought of this Fantasy is making me want this woman! I'll pick this up late, whoa!!

INSTRUCTIONS

Before we begin! Yes I am in touch with my feminine side but don't get it Twisted!! If I could I would build a house in a coochie!! I wrote this right here at 7-9-2011 at, 10:48pm! Now this is what I like done to me by a woman or women. Seduce Me!! Does anyone remember how to do that any more?! You be the huntress and I be your prey! How would you get my attention? If I had company how would you make yourself noticeable to me?! Think and imagine that, I'll wait! Now that you have my attention what do you do to keep it?! How would you leave an impression that lasts until we talk?! How would you steal a Moment with me? I love a woman's touch with soft hands and fingers. Touch me like you touch yourself, through my clothes and all! Rub my bald head like a crystal ball, whisper things that get me aroused. Breathe your sweet hot breath underneath my earlobe. Combine your breath and the touch of your tongue as you go down my neck. Rub my shoulders and arms desiring there embrace as you do so. Look at me with a surprised, excited and intrigued expression as your hands come across the piercing in my chest. Imagine the many ways that you could tantalize and tease with fingers, teeth (No Hard Biting), tongue and lips on it. Run your nails or finger tips gently over my exposed skin and lightly skimming the hairs. Then a peck below my earlobe or maybe a nibble, something to send a tingle down my spine. If all this is done then further instructions will follow. Until then keep practicing. OEK

BOSS LADY, BOSS LADY

Boss lady I see you sexy! With your professional attire complimenting your intriguing frame! No offense but your clothes even though fitting they still do you no justice! I truly mean that! When I told you that I could see you were fine upon entering the office behind you. It went over your head! Even though we may not be each others Fantasy person, there's still something that intrigues us sexually! The only question is just what, it is that's doing it. Whatever it maybe, we both know that one day it may have to be explored. Your preference of man or woman bothers me not! If it's women that you want, then the more the merrier. Now if you want another man, then wash your ass, coochie, mouth and body after your done! Don't for get the protection because it's going to be a long experience! One on one, mmm, mmm, mmm! You got my entire attention! If you could see the look on my face you would be afraid in a lust-full passionate way! You would know by the time that we actually got to the actual act you would've either or was trying not too cum! The crotch of your pant suit or the seat of your skirt is soaked thru the fabric and is staining the seat your on. What's the matter is something I said bothering you right now?! I'm trying to be that late night early mourning need that you want fulfilled and want that needs to be fulfilled! You know what

I'm talking about that thing that she doesn't have. And that thing that he just is not doing correctly! You know what those things are because you are blushing right now at the fact that you know exactly what they are?! Don't you?!

V6

This beautiful woman and her two girlfriends came up to me and said that she was please to meet me. But she still wouldn't tell me her name. okay I believe in mystery, so let's play your game. She was looking for a man to love her, like she'd never been loved before. A man that would do it anywhere even on her limousine floor! What she didn't know that tonight she was in my Fantasy world! And I hope she was a nasty girl! Tonight she will come literally for me, because I like nasty girls! She said she like sailors and I stopped her when I said, look I got coochie on the brain! Your clit on my tongue will make you forget all about them other candy kanes. Now if your not scared pull them thongs too the side, so I can lick you like a lesbian would, but better! Tonight you gone ride my tongue to that land in your Fantasy! Tonight you will say no, don't stop and beg me too! Can you be my nasty girl?! Your moans of passion and pleasure will flow from deep within. YOU can stop wondering if I think you're a nasty girl so much! The answer is no! She didn't like the music playing so she asked could I change the station! When the music that she could flow with came on her whole demeanor changed! She had transformed in front of me. She seemed more aggressive with a lustful passion in her movements and touch. Seductively she moaned that she could no longer hold it. Whatever the hell it was-was catching it tonight! I like to fell out when she said she needed seven inches or more! Oh I got you, I said right before I pushed that ass back up against them seats and proceeded to give her Tongue-Fu and the Two Fingers of Pleasure at the same time! Yeah that ass was stuck to them seats like gravity intensified. One hand grabs a breast the other dug into the seat. Both of her knee high stiletto boots were pressed back and into the cushions. Her eyes rolled up into her head, mouth gaped wide open, mini skirt sits between her plump ass and the cushions. The thigh high stockings with that line up the back got her deeper into than she knew. Not only did I have suction or her clit my tongue is exploring the outer walls of her love tunnel. With my index finger knuckle deep inside her and my middle finger is in her anus. Her head was so twisted that she didn't even know what she was saying! Wake her when I'm done?! She passed out after the fifth time she came . . . . , within the hour! Trust me when I say I was not the only one having fun that night. It just so happened her two other girlfriends saw what went down! Now do you actually think that I really was the only one that was having fun?! Why do you think you were still in the limo this mourning, huh?!

A PEEK INTO MY NEXT BOOK:

The diary of a black hue MAN

FADE INTO THE BACK GROUND

It still doesn't and shouldn't seem to affect me much as the initial shock of the weapon that you made and the choice to use it against me! The age old saying no longer holds the emotions back. The rational FRIEND fades until my presence is only background as I wonder why I came here. The time lost by YOUR pride clearly solidifies the fact of this REALITY! Congratulations on your wedding day! Imagine my shock as the places have now changed. The FRIEND who made the claims to love me and always to be there like that artist sang about. The light at the end of the tunnel slowly forms into your wedding dress. My REALITY played out in this brother's lyrics has me rubbing my eyes, like the video that wasn't shot for this particular song. The only thing is he's watching me deal with the heart breaking situation as though he was the one directing while I performed. That weapon you call pride has blinded you so much that you can't even look me in the eyes that says all that is needed! Our connections went deeper than what we shared together. Not one to cause a scene but nobody notices me throw the bottle back while shouting, "she's with somebody else, because her pride won't allow her to accept her mistake!" The final and nearly fatal blow comes when the painful truth that this song would be playing in our hearts on the day that all I could do was FADE INTO THE BACKGROUND! Thank you for making me a great writer. Tears flow down as gravity pulls the connection that we had apart with the transference of tears that you can't shed. My tears stain the fabric in your heart and mind, with one last congratulatory smile as I stop and turn before I fade. The slight meeting that caused the artist and myself switch back. Two brothers see things from another's perspective and the video ends. Hopefully this time is different maybe the FRIEND will open her eyes before she goes to far and has a hard time finding her way back! To the FRIEND that was and will forever be, my definition of just that. True To Form, she knows who she is!!!

COULD YOU BE?!

My heart still longs for that someone to hold it carefully and lovingly! I often wonder if that person will ever come forward to claim me as theirs one day. Does that person even exist in this world?! A FEMALE FIREND who tries to understand me totally. They can flow as I do without judgment because they know that's not their JOB! We connect on a different level where the impossible is possible and the unthinkable thinkable! Someone to love me unconditionally as my children do! Is that possible?! Yes, it is and that is what I want!! Now if you feel that you're that person then step up and come get it. I'm here with my accepted faults, able to adjust and adapt to my environment, how about you?! If you're ready to flow with the natural flow of my mood then let's flow! I'm waiting . . . , the black hueMAN!!

A DADDY AND PROUD

I've been told that I've embraced fatherhood very well! Sometimes, I wonder about that for many reasons but one stands out the most. The feelings that I have for my children are new and at times overwhelming! To love and have someone love you back unconditionally with a child-like mentality, still innocent to the world. A love that lingers with absence hurts when it leaves and Always like the first time new when it returns. That's a hell of an emotional roller coaster right there! Especially to have to deal with and adjust to something like that on a daily basis. How does someone adjust to that and not be affected in some way form or fashion? All I do is Pray for the stability, mentally and emotionally to keep doing the things that I have to do for my children! My Faith keeps me strong through this and all the other rides on this journey through life. My children are what I was Blessed with and with that comes a even greater, Responsibility!

MY CONDOLENCES

You didn't have to tell me about the pain of your loss, just the fact that you're in pain makes me feel your pain. As a Friend I understand somewhat how you feel, I don't know that person as you did but through you I get a sense as to who they were. The love that you display and share with others is enough to have a good idea of who they were as a person. The influences that they had in your life are shown only to those who pay attention! I feel Blessed to share in the influences that they've had on you to make you the person that you are. Tears fill eyes as my mind wonders at what you miss about that person. I add them to my Prayers for you as I've always done for those who've touched my life as I have touched theirs. Know that I love you and have shed tears for you as you deal with this pain. A Friend, the black hueMAN! For you, Val.

THE WARNING

If the truth will set you free, then why does it hurt so much when told?! You can't handle the truth!! You say that you can but when it's told to you can you handle it?! Think about it for a Moment, and yes I will wait!! You asked me for the truth and that's exactly what you got. Now I know that I have no type of chofe or tact when speaking truthfully. It's not meant to hurt your feelings when I say it but I've already told you that from the start. Acting like this is some new shit is not even going to fly with me because you have already been warned! Don't be mad or upset if you thought that I've changed in my honesty, when you ask me questions. Some questions need not be asked! Just remember I will speak the truth in my own opinion from my own experiences. Now will you be able to handle that?! If you don't want a truthful and honest answer then don't ask me because that's just what it is you're going to get from me damn near every single time you ask! Just be careful as to what it is that you are asking!!